Perfect Puppies

Alfie the Cheeky Puppy

Alfie
the Cheeky Puppy

JULIE SYKES

Illustrated by Lisa Alderson

■SCHOLASTIC

Published in the UK by Scholastic, 2025
Scholastic, Bosworth Avenue, Warwick, CV34 6UQ

SCHOLASTIC and associated logos are trademarks and/or
registered trademarks of Scholastic Inc.

Text © Julie Sykes, 2025
Illustrations by Lisa Alderson © Scholastic, 2025

The moral rights of the author have been asserted by them.

ISBN 978 0702 34054 3

A CIP catalogue record for this book is available from the British Library.

All rights reserved.
This book is sold subject to the condition that it shall not, by way of trade or
otherwise, be lent, hired out or otherwise circulated in any form of binding
or cover other than that in which it is published. No part of this publication
may be reproduced, stored in a retrieval system, or transmitted in any form
or by any other means (electronic, mechanical, photocopying, recording or
otherwise) or used to train any artificial intelligence technologies without prior
written permission of Scholastic Limited. Subject to EU law Scholastic Limited
expressly reserves this work from the text and data mining exception.

Printed in the UK
Paper made from wood grown in sustainable
forests and other controlled sources.

10 9 8 7 6 5 4 3 2 1

This is a work of fiction. Any resemblance to actual people,
events or locales is entirely coincidental.

www.scholastic.co.uk

For safety or quality concerns:
UK: www.scholastic.co.uk/productinformation
EU: www.scholastic.ie/productinformation

For Summer,
who loves a perfect puppy.

CHAPTER 1

Amelia Jones was in the kitchen adding pineapple to a circle of pizza dough when Dad came home.

"Hello, my favourite girls," he said. "Friday pizza and ice-cream night, is it? What a great end to a lovely week."

Mum was preparing a salad, and Dad pinched a cherry tomato before joining Amelia at the worktop.

"Is that all you're having, Amelia? No mushrooms or ham? Not even some extra cheese? You're not ill, are you?"

Amelia wasn't, not unless you counted feeling homesick for her old life as an illness. Dad worked for a company that built houses and a week ago the Joneses had moved to Barkington, where his company had opened a new office. Mum didn't mind where they lived. She could do her job of translating documents into different languages from anywhere.

Amelia was finding it harder to settle. Her new school was much bigger and noisier than her old one. She missed her friends and didn't know how to make new ones. Feeling Mum and Dad's eyes on her, Amelia bravely added more grated cheese to her pizza.

"How was school, Amelia?" asked Dad as he piled ham and pepperoni on to a pizza base.

"Kelly seems nice," said Amelia carefully.

Everyone liked Kelly. Amelia wished they could be friends, but Kelly was already best friends with Anushka and Jack.

"The first week is always the hardest. I'm sure it won't be long before Amelia has settled in," said Mum kindly. "Granny and Grandpa moved house when I was a similar age and, just like you, I had to start a new school halfway through the term." Mum's eyes misted over as she remembered. "I had a little dog back then called Bonny. She made me feel much braver. I used to walk Bonny to school, and when we arrived, I had the confidence to go in on my own."

"Then maybe we could get Amelia a dog," said Dad as he added tomato and sweetcorn to his pizza.

"That's a great idea," said Mum. "A dog would boost your confidence, Amelia. Everyone in my class said hello to Bonny and it helped me to talk to them."

"It would also be a lot more fun exploring Barkington with a puppy," Dad added.

Amelia thought about it. Could a puppy really help her to feel less lonely? "Maybe," she said warily.

"What sort of dog would you like?" asked Mum.

Amelia didn't answer. She wasn't actually sure that she wanted a dog. Bouncy ones made her nervous and so did the barky ones. Granny had a quiet cat who purred when she sat on Amelia's lap. Perhaps she should get a cat instead.

"We could look for a dog this weekend if you'd like to?" continued Mum.

Amelia half nodded, neither agreeing nor disagreeing.

"Great idea," said Dad, balancing some olives on his sweetcorn. "I've finished. My pizza is ready to go in the oven!"

"Careful, Robert, or the toppings will fall off," Mum said. "Your dinner looks more like the Leaning Tower of Pisa than a pizza! Have you finished, Amelia? Can I cook yours now?"

Mum put the pizzas in the oven and Amelia laid the table. Soon the kitchen was filled with the rich smell of melting cheese.

Mum got out her iPad and started scrolling through it. "Come and look at these puppy pictures, Amelia. Aren't they cute?"

Amelia's tummy tightened as she looked over Mum's shoulder. The puppies were adorable, but Amelia wanted a friend. Could that friend be a dog?

CHAPTER 2

The following morning, Amelia's parents didn't mention dogs again.

They must have forgotten about getting me one, thought Amelia. While she was mostly relieved, a small part of her was a tiny bit disappointed. After a delicious breakfast of a warm croissant filled with scrambled eggs washed down with a mug of hot chocolate, Amelia was ready to go exploring.

"It's a glorious day now that the rain has stopped. Let's walk into Barkington," Dad suggested.

Barkington was in the opposite direction to Amelia's school. Feeling light-headed with happiness that she had two whole days off, Amelia ran ahead of her parents, leaping over the puddles. They cut through a park with a pond and a cycle trail through some woods. The town centre was modern with a big shopping complex, a cinema and places to eat. As they walked past the cinema, Amelia saw an easel-like board. On it, in shouty capital letters, it was advertising:

"I'm nine," Amelia said to herself. The cinema club looked like good fun. Suddenly Amelia heard voices that she recognized. She spun round and there was Kelly with her best friends, Anushka and Jack. They were hurrying into the cinema with a grown-up.

"Would you like to go to cinema club?" Dad asked loudly.

The tips of Amelia's ears turned pink as Kelly, Anushka and Jack turned to see who was shouting. Amelia looked away quickly. The Saturday Morning Cinema Club sounded fun, but she couldn't go in on her own, especially not now when Dad was being so embarrassing.

"No thanks," she mumbled.

Amelia followed her parents through the town centre. They reached a path that led to a river.

Mum's eyes lit up. "Look at the boats and the swans. Let's walk along the towpath."

As Amelia walked, she admired the boats and the swans gliding along the river. To the side of the towpath was a field speckled with wild flowers and bushes. The family hadn't gone far when a golden dog bounded across it. It had a long pink tongue and hot, panty breath.

The dog went up to Amelia and nudged her hand.

"Hello," said Amelia awkwardly.

"Isn't she pretty!" cooed Mum.

The dog was pale gold with a white stripe that ran from the top of her head to the tip of her nose. She had triangular-shaped ears that flopped over, a white chest and four white paws. Round her neck she wore a yellow collar patterned with red hearts. A bone-shaped metal disc hung from the collar. The dog sat down on the towpath and stared up at Amelia expectantly.

"Excuse me," Amelia said politely. "Please can you move."

The dog stayed where she was, and Amelia had to step round her, but as she walked on with her parents, the dog followed them.

"Oh dear," said Mum after a while. "She

must be lost. She's wearing a dog tag. It should have the owner's phone number on it." Mum reached out to look, but the dog bounced away and into the field. Then she stopped, wagged her tail and barked playfully.

"Stay!" said Mum firmly. She took a step forward, but the dog jumped out of reach again.

Amelia watched as the dog drew Mum into the field, woofing then darting away each time Mum got too close.

"She wants us to follow her," said Amelia suddenly.

"I think you're right," said Dad. "This way – let's see where she's taking us."

The dog opened her mouth in what Amelia decided was a friendly smile before scampering off across the field.

Occasionally she would stop and look back to check that Amelia and her family were still there.

The field ended at a road, and a short way along it was a drive that curved away. A large sign hung from the open gate.

"*The Paw Pad*," Amelia read aloud. "*A pawsome place for Perfect Puppies.*" Underneath was a picture of a multicoloured paw.

The dog headed up the drive. Amelia heard voices coming her way and a tall, slim lady with short blonde hair came into view. She was wearing jeans and a pink-and-blue sweatshirt. The sweatshirt had a coloured paw print on it like the one on the sign. A younger man, who looked the same age as Amelia's parents, was with her. He wore shiny shoes, smart jeans, an open-neck shirt and a casual jacket.

The lady's voice was steely. "Thank you for calling in again, Mr Kat, but my answer is still the same. The Paw Pad is *not* for sale."

Mr Kat scowled, then suddenly he noticed Amelia and her parents. "Thank you for your time, Mrs Springer," he said politely. He smiled, showing off his dazzling white teeth as he nodded at Amelia's parents.

Amelia shivered as Mr Kat strode away. His smile had felt as friendly as a hungry tiger.

Mrs Springer's face relaxed. "Hello, my lovelies," she said warmly to Amelia and her parents. "I'm Mrs Springer. Welcome to the Paw Pad, a *pawsome* place for Perfect Puppies."

Amelia glanced at her parents suspiciously. Mrs Springer didn't seem surprised to see them. Had her parents arranged to come here?

The dog gave a sharp bark. Mrs Springer grinned, "I run the Paw Pad with the help of my faithful friend Lucky, of course."

"Lucky sounds like she understands you," said Mum, laughing as she bent to stroke her.

Mrs Springer nodded. "Lucky is a very special dog. One night, many years ago when I was feeling very alone, I found her on my doorstep. She was so tiny and all she had with her was a collar and lead and a pretty paw-shaped stone."

"So you kept her?" asked Dad.

"Lucky filled a hole in my life and we became the best of friends. Then one day she disappeared. I was frantic with worry, but as I set out to look for her, would you believe who met me on the drive? Lucky and another small puppy wearing a collar and lead. Not long after that, I met a young mother with a new baby who was struggling to entertain her active older son. The new puppy loved ball games, and the boy and dog became inseparable. Since then, the puppies – and the

children who need them – keep arriving at the Paw Pad."

"How interesting," said Mum, glancing meaningfully at Dad. "It feels like Lucky brought us here, too. We're Susan and Robert Jones, and this is our daughter, Amelia. We were only saying last night that it would be great if we could get Amelia a puppy."

Mrs Springer's kind green eyes held Amelia's for a moment. A warm feeling spread through Amelia. For a second, it felt as though Mrs Springer could see right through her and knew just how hard she found it to make friends.

Then Mrs Springer smiled. "Would you like to come and have a look around? Who knows … you might even find your perfect puppy."

CHAPTER 3

Amelia's tummy fizzed with excitement.

Lucky came and sat on her feet, and Mrs Springer's gaze switched to the dog. "Lucky likes you. She doesn't sit on anyone's toes. She definitely thinks we have your perfect puppy."

Amelia glowed with pride, even though she knew that Mrs Springer was teasing her. How could Lucky know that? And, anyway, Amelia still wasn't sure whether she wanted a puppy. Lucky gave her a gentle nudge, as if to say, *Yes, you do!*

"A beagle would be nice," said Mum. "Beagles are good family dogs and they are easy to groom."

"They also need long walks and they like chasing things," Dad pointed out. "How about an Old English sheepdog? They are very cuddly and they don't need as much exercise."

"Old English sheepdogs are huge when they're fully grown," Mum exclaimed. "And they need a lot of grooming. How about a Scottie?

Mrs Springer led them down the drive. At the end, on one side was a small cottage and on the other a low building with a sloping roof. It had a blue-and-pink door with a sign above it welcoming everyone to the Paw Pad. Mrs Springer shepherded everyone into a large reception area that had a bone-shaped desk. On the desk was a computer and a jar of dog treats. The walls were hung with canvas pictures of happy-looking dogs and there was a display board overflowing with more photographs of dogs and their owners. Set in the wall behind the desk, in a glass box, was a paw-shaped stone that glimmered softly.

The stone that Lucky arrived with, thought Amelia, and for some reason it made her feel happy.

On the floor was a potted plant with huge glossy green leaves and beside it was a metal bowl of water and a dog bed. Lucky went over and flopped down on the bed.

"Are the dogs through there?" Dad

pointed at two doors. One was pink and the other blue and they were both covered in tiny sketches of dogs. The pink door was labelled the **LEAD ROOM**.

Mrs Springer smiled. "They are. If you would both like to have a seat, you can browse the *Paw Post* – it's our journal and it showcases our success stories. Lucky's in there too. Amelia, you come with me. Here at the Paw Pad, we let the puppies decide on the perfect puppy for our visitors."

Amelia glanced at her parents. Discovering the Paw Pad by chance seemed much too convenient. She was certain now that they had secretly arranged to visit the Paw Pad. She waited awkwardly while Mrs Springer brought them drinks and a copy of the *Paw Post*.

Mrs Springer's eyes sparkled as she turned to Amelia. "It's time to find you a puppy."

Stiffly, Amelia followed Mrs Springer through the door marked **LEAD ROOM**. *Where are the puppies?* Amelia wondered, looking around as the door closed behind her. All she could see was a room full of dog leads. Her eyes widened as they travelled over the pale blue walls covered in hooks shaped like dog tails. The room was filled with racks, also with more dog-tail-shaped hooks, and dog leads hanging from them. Red, orange, yellow and green – there was every colour you could imagine and more.

On the ceiling, paw-shaped coloured lights shone down, making a pattern of swirling paw prints on the floor. Amelia relaxed as a new feeling washed over her. It was hard to describe. It felt as if she was full of bubbles and it made her dizzy with excitement and happiness.

"Do you like it?" asked Mrs Springer.

"I love it!" Amelia gasped.

"Amelia Jones," said Mrs Springer solemnly. "Answer me carefully. Do you want a puppy?"

Amelia hesitated, then the answer burst from inside her: "YES!"

Mrs Springer stared at her for a long

moment before speaking. "Do you believe in magic?"

That question was much easier to answer! "Yes," said Amelia.

Mrs Springer smiled. "Then I'm going to have to ask you to keep a big magical secret. The Paw Pad is no ordinary place but a magic one. The magic comes from the stone that Lucky brought with her. It can pair a person like you with their perfect puppy, but only if that person promises not to tell the secret to anyone. Can you do that for me?"

Amelia felt like she might burst with joy. She'd sensed there was something special about the paw-shaped stone. She also knew that magic was real, no matter how often some of her friends said it wasn't.

"I won't tell," she said breathlessly.

Mrs Springer said kindly. "Walk around the leads without touching any, and think about the type of puppy that you'd like as your best friend.

Amelia looked around in wonder. *Is this place actually magic? Will the lead room be able to help me?* she wondered. *Do I really want a puppy or do I just want new friends?* Amelia thought of her old classmates. She wanted her new friends to be like them: kind, funny, generous. Friends who wouldn't judge, even when you messed up. Friends who were there for you always.

"WOOF!"

Amelia almost jumped out of her shoes as a deep pink lead decorated with sparkly gold bones barked at her.

"WOOF!" barked the lead again in a friendly way, as if it was asking to be patted.

Amelia couldn't resist. Before she knew it, her hand was stroking the lead. It was warm and as soft as dog fur. It nuzzled into her and then it licked her with a rough, wet tongue.

"Whoa!" She must have imagined that. Leads were not warm and hairy and they did not lick people.

The lead gave a happy bark, then it leapt off its hook and into Amelia's hand. She just had time to notice that the brown tail-shaped hook was long with short smooth fur, before Mrs Springer swooped down on her.

"Congratulations," she said with a smile. "You are one paw-step away from finding your perfect puppy. Are you ready?"

Amelia was filled with a warm glow. "I am."

Mrs Springer opened a door. "This way."

They went through it and came to an outside courtyard with a huge rectangle of grass filled with play equipment. The grass was bordered on three sides by luxurious kennels each with its own separate sleeping area.

"A doggie play park!" Amelia exclaimed. She giggled as a chocolate-brown Labrador with a muscular tail jumped on to the see-saw and the tiny Yorkie sitting on the other end bounced up in the air.

A black-and-white Border collie chased an identical puppy in and out of a line of poles. Their ears were flapping, their eyes were focused and their tails

streamed behind them like kites. A golden Labradoodle with too-big paws kept swatting a box, trying to release the ball from inside it.

Amelia's tummy fluttered anxiously. There were so many puppies – which one was hers? Then Amelia saw her perfect puppy.

CHAPTER 4

The pretty apricot-coloured cockapoo with big brown eyes was hiding under the slide. Shyly, she watched the other puppies as they played. Amelia recognized that look. The puppy wanted to join in, but she couldn't find the courage. Amelia often felt like that. Understanding rushed through her. The cockapoo had to be her perfect puppy. Tightly holding the pink-and-gold lead, Amelia walked over to the slide. She was almost there when the Labrador puppy saw her. He jumped off the see-saw, but his legs went one way and his body the other. He flopped on to the grass, lying on his back with his paws paddling the air. Scrambling up, he bounded over to Amelia, barrelling into her legs.

"Ooomph!" she squeaked.

Excited by the noise, the Labrador puppy jumped up at her, his tiny claws pricking into Amelia's legs. Amelia looked to Mrs Springer for help. Then something magical happened. The pink-and-gold lead warmed in her hand and glowed.

Mrs Springer beamed with delight. "This is Alfie. See how his collar matches your lead? Congratulations Amelia, you've found your perfect puppy."

"No!" Amelia pushed away the slobbery over-enthusiastic puppy. "There's been a mistake. This puppy is too bouncy." She glanced over at the cockapoo, who had now settled down for a nap.

"The magic never fails," said Mrs Springer. "The lead and collar match.

Alfie's just excited to meet you. Stand still and ignore him until he calms down. Then you can crouch to his height to say hello."

Nervously, Amelia did as she was told and stood still. After a short while, Alfie stopped jumping up at her. Feeling more confident, Amelia squatted to his height.

"Hello, Alfie," she whispered.

Alfie went wild with excitement nudging Amelia's hand with his head and resting his paws on her bent legs. Amelia was overwhelmed and a little scared.

"Please," she said. "Can you stop jumping on me?"

"Alfie, off," said Mrs Springer firmly. Alfie ignored her and jumped up again. "Off," Mrs Springer repeated.

To Amelia's surprise, Alfie stopped jumping at her. Mrs Springer pulled a soft dog treat from her pocket and offered it to the puppy on a flat palm. Alfie gobbled it up, then looked at Mrs Springer with adoring eyes.

"Good boy!" she praised him. Then she turned to Amelia. "Use one-word commands. And praise is important. Praise with your voice and, while they are still learning, always give them a treat."

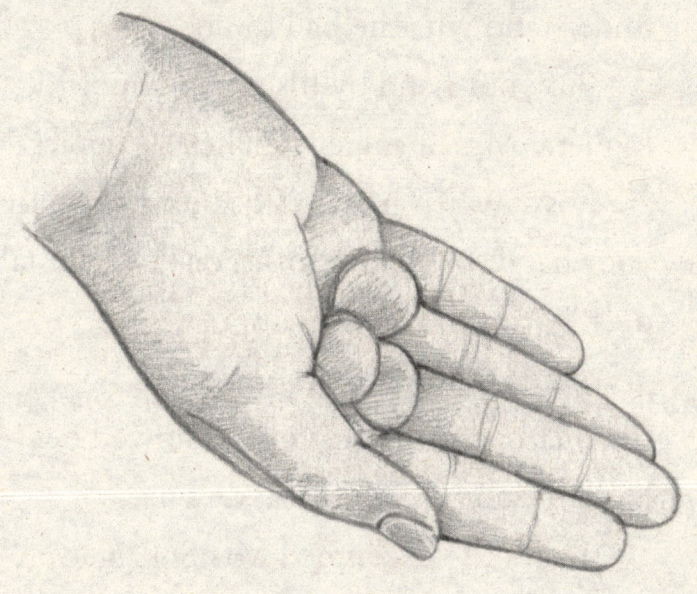

Mrs Springer pulled a handful of small, round discs from her pocket and gave them to Amelia. "Here. Alfie loves these. Now try telling him to sit."

Amelia's nose curled up. The dog treats were pongy, but Alfie's eyes hadn't left Amelia's hand.

"Sit," she said hesitantly.

Alfie stared up at her, as if he didn't understand what he had to do.

"Put your hand by his nose, then lift it higher," Mrs Springer told her. "Puppies are nosy. When he raises his head to follow your hand, he'll have to sit, or else he'll fall over."

Amelia followed Mrs Springer's instructions. As Alfie's eyes followed her hand, he automatically sat down.

"That's it!" exclaimed Mrs Springer.

"Tell him he's a good boy and give him a treat."

"Good boy," said Amelia, popping a treat into Alfie's mouth and suddenly feeling much happier.

"Put his lead on," said Mrs Springer. "Then when he's said goodbye to his playmates, you can take him home."

With fumbling fingers, Amelia clipped the pink-and-gold lead to Alfie's collar. She led him around the grass, letting him touch noses with all the other puppies. Alfie walked nicely and Amelia felt a flash of pride.

The feeling didn't last for long…

They followed Mrs Springer through a different door, along a corridor and through a blue door, entering the reception area. Mr and Mrs Jones were side by side, their heads touching. They were still reading the *Paw*

Post. Excitement danced in Amelia's tummy as she prepared to show them her new puppy. Alfie yapped excitedly, then charged towards them, knocking into the plant pot. Amelia gasped as the pot wobbled and, with a crash, tipped over spewing earth across the clean floor.

Alfie yelped, then skittered away. He slid on the floor, but then he lost control of his large paws and trod on the edge of the water bowl. Water flooded across the room, splashing Lucky. She leapt out of her bed, stalked to the opposite side of the room and sat down, but Amelia was sure from the sparkle in her eyes that she was laughing.

Alfie had a blob of mud on his nose. He dived at Amelia's parents and shook himself vigorously, splattering them with muddy droplets of water. Then he wiped his face on their legs.

"Oh, Amelia, he's adorable!" Dad chuckled.

Mum laughed so much that tears ran down her face. Amelia didn't find it even a teensy bit funny. Her face burned with embarrassment. Why was Alfie her perfect puppy and not the shy cockapoo? How could Mrs Springer be sure that the magic was never wrong?

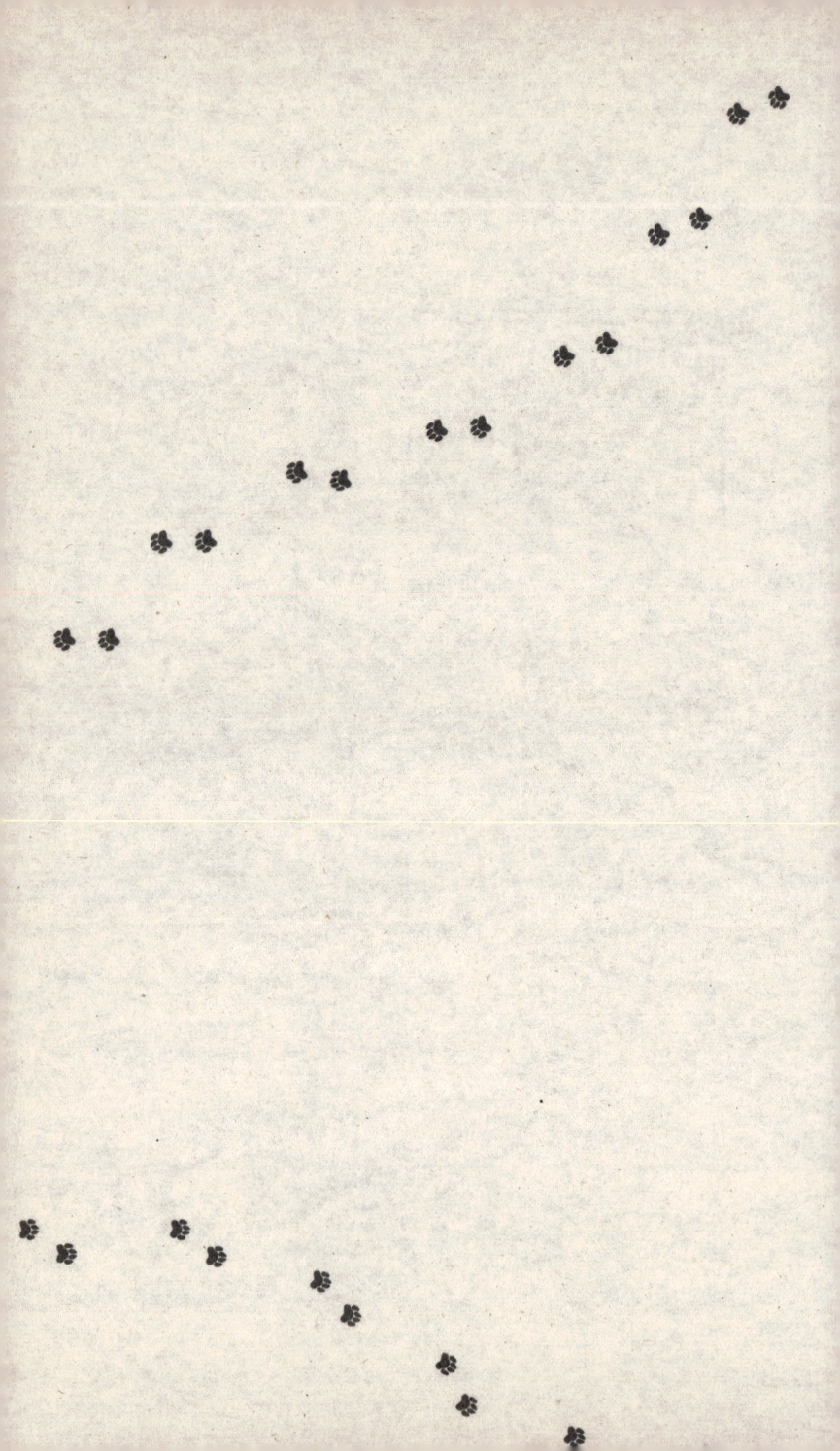

CHAPTER 5

Mrs Springer picked up the plant pot and the empty water bowl.

"Don't worry about the mud," she said cheerfully. She went behind the reception desk and returned with a huge roll of paper, which she used to blot it.

"Alfie, no!" she added as the cheeky puppy dived at the paper and began to shred it. "Take him away so he can't reach it," she told Amelia.

Amelia tried to guide
Alfie away, but, apart from selecting her
supposedly perfect puppy, the lead didn't
seem to have any other magical properties.
Alfie pounced on another piece of paper
and scooted off with his prize. Amelia
tightened her grip as Alfie dragged her

along. This was no good. Alfie wouldn't stop, even when she pulled on his lead. She didn't have a clue how else to get him to do as she needed.

"Alfie, stop. Put the paper down and walk nicely," Amelia pleaded.

"Alfie, leave!" said Mrs Springer firmly.

Approaching Alfie, she held out a treat in one hand. Immediately, Alfie dropped the paper. Mrs Springer picked it up while handing him the treat. "Good boy!"

"Don't look so sad," said Mrs Springer. "Alfie just needs training. I'll give you the details of the nearest puppy classes. Once he's settled in, you might like to check them out. Now, I just need to get your parents to fill in a boring form before you leave."

Dad and Mum stood up and went over to

her desk. Dad took a card out of his wallet.

"How much do we owe you for Alfie?" he asked.

"There's no charge," said Mrs Springer. "Some people make a donation, but only give if you can. The money is used for running the Paw Pad."

Amelia was still having second thoughts about taking Alfie home with her. Was it too late to change her mind? Before she could gather up the courage to tell her parents that she didn't want a puppy after all, it was too late and she was leaving the Paw Pad with a very bouncy Alfie.

Mrs Springer, with Lucky by her side, waved them goodbye. "Good luck! Send pictures to let me how you're both getting on."

Alfie was too excited to walk straight.

He kept biting the lead and trying to tug it from Amelia's hands. Mum and Dad were no help at all, laughing loudly as Amelia became tangled up. Alfie loved the puddles – the bigger and muddier, the better. He kept sprinting forward, dragging Amelia behind him as he jumped in them.

"Alfie! You're splashing me," squealed Amelia. Soon, her jeans were soaked and muddy.

She felt hot with embarrassment as she and her parents approached the town centre. It was busy and people were staring at her and Alfie.

The Saturday Morning Cinema Club had just finished and a stream of children were leaving the building. Amelia's heart sank further. She hunched her shoulders, making herself smaller, and stared at the ground, ignoring everyone, even the children who were calling out things like, "Look at the cute puppy."

Alfie loved the attention. Without warning, he changed direction, towing Amelia with him as he went to say hello to a boy munching on a carton of popcorn.

"Alfie, no!" Amelia tripped over the cinema's display board.

With an ear-splitting screech, it slid across the ground. People turned to look and giggle. Amelia's cheeks went pink as she tried to stop Alfie from stealing the boy's popcorn. At last, Mum came to Amelia's rescue, firmly telling Alfie to leave and helping Amelia to walk him back to her father.

Dad was deep in conversation with a man. His face lit up as Mum and Amelia came closer. "Susan, Amelia, I'd like you to meet Colin. We work together."

When everyone had said hello and Alfie had licked and jumped on Colin, Amelia drifted over to a nearby bench to wait while the grown-ups finished talking. Glumly, she realized she'd made a huge mistake. Alfie was not helping her to fit in. Instead, he was making her stand out and not in a good way. Amelia decided that when her parents stopped talking, she'd ask them to take Alfie back.

A man came and sat on the bench next to Amelia's, whispering into his mobile. Amelia frowned. She recognized him from the Paw Pad. She was intrigued and, even though she knew it was rude, she couldn't help but listen.

"Yes," said the man, nodding vigorously. "I need the leaflets to be ready by tomorrow, Sunday. Everyone who wants to become the mayor of Barkington is giving a speech at the Picnic in the Park event. I shall talk about all the free stuff people will get if they vote for me, like parking, popcorn at the cinema and ice creams at the weekend."

The man listened to the person on the other end of the phone and his face lit up with a smile.

"Exactly! And then when I'm the mayor, I'll close the Paw Pad down. How? Easy, I'll raise taxes so high that Mrs Springer won't be able to afford them. She'll be

finally forced to sell it to me." He laughed unpleasantly. "I hate dogs! Nasty, smelly, slobbery animals. I'm going to turn the Paw Pad into the Purrfect Palace, a luxury hotel for cats. Mr Kat, that's me – and *Kats* are better than dogs!"

Mr Kat cackled as he ended the call and stood up, scowling at Alfie, who was chewing on the leg of the bench.

Amelia couldn't breathe. Mr Kat was planning to close the Paw Pad. But what about Mrs Springer and all her puppies? Where would they live? And what would happen to the wonderful magical lead room?

CHAPTER 6

Amelia sprang up. She had to get to the Paw Pad immediately and warn Mrs Springer. Mum and Dad had finished talking and Amelia hurried over. Alfie thought they were playing a game and he jumped at Amelia's legs as she ran.

"Alfie, down!" Amelia almost fell over him. "Mum, Dad," she gabbled, her words spilling out.

"Woof!" Alfie barked loudly. He wagged his tail, excited by the noise he was making. "Woof, woof, WOOF!"

The louder Amelia talked, the louder Alfie barked. In her frustration, Amelia nearly stamped a foot. It was almost as if Alfie was deliberately barking over her.

"It's about the Paw Pad!" she bellowed just as Alfie fell silent.

Her parents stared at her in surprise. "What about the Paw Pad?" asked Mum.

Alfie fixed Amelia with a fierce stare and sat down hard on her foot. It really was as if he was trying to tell her something. Then, with a jolt, Mrs Springer's words came back to Amelia. The Paw Pad and its magical lead room had to be kept a secret. Amelia panicked and she hung her head unsure how to continue.

Mum and Dad waited expectantly.

"What is it, honey?" asked Mum gently.

Amelia blinked. "Er… I liked the Paw Pad and Mrs Springer was really nice. Wouldn't it be horrible if anything

happened and the Paw Pad had to shut? Where would all the puppies stay then?"

Mum and Dad exchanged a confused look.

"That man we saw. On the drive," said Amelia, trying again.

Dad's face cleared. "Mrs Springer told him that the Paw Pad wasn't for sale. That was obvious. Mrs Springer is much too fond of dogs," said Dad. Changing the subject, he said, "Colin was telling us about Picnic in the Park tomorrow. It's a community event with a stage for people to perform on. There's a dog show, dancing and live music. How would you like to go?"

"I've got some of your favourite picky bits in the freezer: spring rolls, samosas and tiny quiches. I can cook them and we can eat them cold," Mum added.

The picnic sounded fun and Mr Kat would be there too, giving his speech. A brilliant idea wiggled into Amelia's head. There was no need to worry Mrs Springer about his plan. Not if she found a way of stopping Mr Kat by herself.

"You and Alfie can enter the dog show," said Mum. "There's a class for the dog and owner who most look like each other."

"I don't look like Alfie!" Amelia said, horrified.

"You've both got brown hair," said Dad.

"I know what we can do," Mum mused. "We'll give Alfie a bath and tomorrow you can both wear matching outfits. Perhaps we could add a clip-on bow to Alfie's collar and you can wear one too."

On the way home, they called in at a pet shop to stock up with all the things that

Alfie needed. Mum and Dad staggered home with several bags.

"I can't wait to try out the strawberry shampoo," Mum said. "It smells so good."

★★★

Alfie did not like being put in the bath. He licked the strawberry shampoo off, then he sneezed loudly as he spat it out. When Mum put the shower hose on him, he bit and shook it, splattering Mum and Amelia and giving them bubble moustaches and beards.

"Alfie!" shrieked Amelia. The spray hose spun round and blasted her in the face with warm water. Soon, Amelia was much soggier than Alfie.

Best of all, Alfie liked Amelia's collection of bath ducks. He batted them with a paw, making even more mess. Mum grabbed

a towel and wiped away the bubbles on Amelia's nose. She lifted Alfie out of the bath, wrapped him in the towel and handed him to Amelia. Then she went downstairs, leaving Amelia to dry a wriggly Alfie.

"Please, stay still," Amelia begged. Alfie licked her face.

"Ew!" Amelia wasn't in the mood to be licked with a slobbery dog tongue.

Grumpily, she carried Alfie downstairs. Mum was recovering at the kitchen table, her damp hair plastered to her face. Dad was making mugs of tea.

"Who's a smart boy?" Mum cooed as Amelia carried in a squirming Alfie.

With aching arms, Amelia put Alfie on the floor, where he immediately made a different kind of puddle.

"Oh dear!" Mum said, laughing.

"Can you do it love? I'm busy with the tea. There's a cloth, gloves and a bucket under the sink," Dad told Amelia.

Amelia held her breath as she put on gloves to mop up the puddle. Her damp clothes were sticking to her and she felt cold and miserable. If this was life with a puppy, then she definitely didn't want one. Alfie had crawled under the table. He stopped gnawing at the table leg to give her a toothy grin.

"Alfie, no. That's naughty!" Amelia pulled him away.

"What's he up to now?" said Mum. "Whoops! Thank goodness the table isn't new." She lifted her mug up to hide her smile.

Amelia breathed deeply. "Mum, Dad!" she blurted out. "I've decided that I don't want a puppy. Can we take Alfie back to the Paw Pad?"

"But we've only just got him," said Dad.

Mum put her mug down. "What's this all about, my lovely?" she asked.

"Woof!" said Alfie quietly, as if he wanted to hear why as well. He stopped chewing and rested his nose on his paws. His eyes were huge and sad as he stared up at Amelia.

Filled with guilt, Amelia looked away. Had she been too hard on Alfie? After all, he was only a puppy. Without thinking, she leaned down to stroke him. Alfie licked her hand, making her feel even worse.

"He's so naughty…" Amelia faltered as she remembered Mr Kat. If he succeeded in becoming mayor, then Alfie wouldn't have a home at the Paw Pad either.

"He's still a baby," said Mum. "How about we have a chat with Mrs Springer and see what she says about taking Alfie back?"

Amelia swallowed hard. "OK."

"That's my girl." Mum ruffled her hair. "I expect the Paw Pad will be closed tomorrow, so we'll speak to her after the weekend."

Alfie looked sleepy. It was hardly surprising after such a busy day. Amelia carried him over to his dog bed. Alfie licked her hand and thumped his tail, as if to say thank you. His eyes closed and, not long after, he began to snuffle and snore. Amelia smothered a giggle as she stroked the top of his silky head. He really was a cutie, if only he could stop getting into so much mischief.

CHAPTER 7

Sunday morning was sunny and dry, the perfect weather for a picnic.

"That's everything," said Mum, cramming a water bowl for Alfie into a rucksack bulging with tasty picnic food and drinks. "You and Alfie look very smart in your matching bows," she added.

"They look like twins," Dad teased.

Self-consciously, Amelia touched the

pink-and-gold bow in her hair. Would people think she looked silly and laugh at her? She was about to pull it out when she caught Mum watching her. Mum had been delighted when she'd bought two stick-on bows at the pet shop the day before. Amelia let her hand drop.

Alfie was better on the lead, but he still pulled a lot. Amelia's arm was aching when they arrived at the park. A stage had been set up with a tent behind it where the performers could wait in private. The park was filling up with people. Amelia spotted Kelly, Anushka, Jack and their families setting out a picnic. There was lots of laughter as everyone helped to unpack a mountain of food. Kelly looked up and, seeing Amelia, she waved. Amelia looked away quickly, her cheeks burning because she'd been caught staring again.

"Shall we sit here?" said Mum, who had also spotted Kelly waving.

"No." Amelia kept walking, but Alfie had smelt food. Spinning round, he dragged Amelia back to Kelly.

"Alfie, not that way. Stop!" Amelia squeaked.

"A puppy! Is he yours?" Kelly put out her hand to say hello, but Alfie ran past her towards the food. Using his nose, he expertly flipped open the lid of a container and pulled out a sausage.

"Alfie, leave!" said Amelia desperately.

Alfie ate faster, munching on the stolen sausage and swallowing it in one big gulp. He went back for another one, but Kelly lifted the container out of the way. Her eyes danced with laughter, but Amelia was too embarrassed to notice.

"I'm sorry," she mumbled.

"Your bows match," said Kelly, giggling. "Cute!"

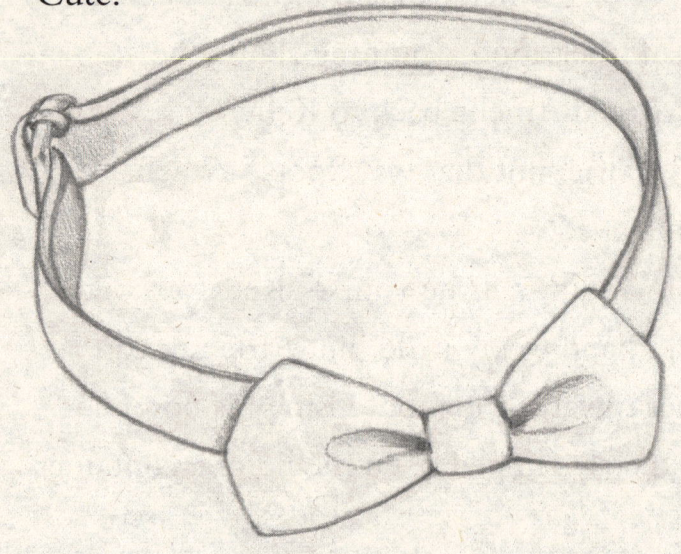

Anushka and Jack couldn't stop laughing. Amelia grew more flustered, certain that they were laughing at her. She pulled Alfie back to her parents, ignoring Kelly who was calling after her.

"Alfie, naughty!" Amelia scolded him. How would she ever make friends if Alfie kept misbehaving!

Amelia's parents picked a grassy spot in front of the stage to eat their picnic. The food was delicious, but Amelia was too upset to eat. She didn't want to enter the dog show. People would only giggle at the matching bows.

"Is that the man we saw at Mrs Springer's yesterday?" Dad asked.

Amelia looked up. Mr Kat was walking briskly towards the tent at the back of the stage.

Mum nodded. "There are only two people standing to be mayor and he's one of them. The speeches must be about to start. Are you ready to go, Amelia? The dog show is straight after."

Amelia jumped up. She'd forgotten all about Mr Kat and she still didn't have any idea how to stop his evil plan. Maybe, if she hung around the tent, something might come to her.

"Please behave," she said to Alfie.

"These might help," said Mum, handing Amelia some dog treats.

Amelia put them in her pocket. Lots of people were hanging out in the back of stage tent. Amelia watched a man show Mr Kat how to use a microphone.

"Stop fussing," Mr Kat told him sternly. "My plan is working. The leaflets you made were great. Lots of people have said they will vote for me."

Amelia felt anger burning inside her. Mr Kat was nothing but a cheat. She had to stop him from tricking the people of Barkington and stealing Mrs Springer's, and her dogs', home. Alfie didn't seem to like Mr Kat either. Suddenly he darted forward, pulling his lead from Amelia's hand as he rammed into the back of Mr Kat's legs. Mr Kat stumbled and, quick as a flash, Alfie snatched the microphone from him and ran away with it.

"Give that back!" roared Mr Kat.

Amelia was frozen with fear as she watched Mr Kat bearing down on Alfie. She didn't want Alfie to get hurt. She ran over to them, then pulled out a dog treat and held it out.

"Alfie, leave," she said firmly.

Alfie hesitated, then dropped the microphone. He let Amelia swap it for the treat.

Mr Kat strode over, his face as squishy and red as a tomato. "I'll take that," he snapped. Shaking with anger, he thrust out a hand.

An idea came to Amelia that made her feel dizzy. What if she turned the microphone on before she gave it back? If Mr Kat continued to tell his assistant about his plans for the Paw Pad, then everyone else would hear. Amelia hesitated. Mr Kat was already furious. How would he react if he saw her do it? Timidly, she stepped back.

"Little girl, give me the microphone." Mr Kat loomed over her.

Something snapped inside Amelia. Firstly, she was not a little girl. Secondly, she remembered all the other puppies at the Paw Pad. Didn't she owe it to them — and to Alfie who would soon be rejoining them — to save their home? Defiantly, Amelia slid the microphone's switch to *ON* before handing it back. She caught a lady watching her.

A second later, Mr Kat's voice boomed over the park. "*I hate dogs, nasty smelly creatures. When I'm mayor, I'll turn the Paw Pad into a luxurious cat hotel…*"

In the tent, Mr Kat's face sagged in horror as he realized his words were echoing around the park. Recovering quickly, he ran on stage.

"Ha ha ha! If you could see your faces. I'm joking, naturally. I'm Mr Kat. A sense of humour is one of the key qualities I could bring to the role as your mayor…"

Mr Kat went on promising the town wonderful things if they voted for him. When he finished speaking, the audience stood up to clap. He strutted off stage like a rock star.

"The cat's in the bag," he said smugly to his assistant. "Or should that be *Kat*?"

The second person wanting to be mayor gave her speech. She didn't have anything free to offer and when she'd finished there was a polite smattering of applause. Mr Kat had won. Everyone would vote for him and then he would take over the Paw Pad and close it down. Amelia hugged Alfie.

"It's time for the dog show. First up is the owner and dog who look most alike. That must be you, my lovely." The lady who Amelia had noticed watching her ushered Alfie and her on to the stage.

There were lots of competitors. Amelia hung at the back, but Alfie dragged her forward and the audience laughed. The lady who'd told Amelia to go on stage was also the judge. She went round with

a microphone, asking each person to explain how they were like their dog. Amelia listened while people talked about the likenesses they shared with their dogs – jumping over logs, dancing in the rain, being scared of spiders.

Too soon, it was Amelia's turn. Her stomach wibbled and wobbled, what would she say? Then suddenly she knew. Taking a very deep breath to stop her hands and voice from shaking, Amelia spoke clearly into the microphone.

"Alfie and I are most like each other because…" Amelia faltered. Did she really have enough courage to speak out?

Alfie thrust his nose into Amelia's free hand. She glanced at him and he gazed back at her adoringly, telling her that she did have enough courage.

Amelia swallowed. "We know about Mr Kat." Her voice was shaky, but undeterred she ploughed on. "We found out what he's planning to do if he becomes your mayor." The words tumbled out faster as Amelia explained what she'd overheard.

When she'd finished, no one spoke. Amelia saw Kelly, Anushka and Jack, watching her with their mouths open in astonishment. Then someone burst out laughing and everyone joined in.

CHAPTER 8

"It's true!" said Amelia, but no one was listening.

Tears prickled behind her eyes. She hung her head. She'd failed. She was about to leave the stage, but Alfie wouldn't let her. He sat on her feet and nudged her hand with his nose again and again, until finally she looked at him. He stared up at her and his big brown eyes were soft with love.

Amelia sniffed and bit her lip. She had to be brave for Alfie and for the other puppies who wouldn't have the Paw Pad to stay at if Mr Kat became mayor. Filled with a new determination, she tried again.

"It's true," she told the crowd firmly.

Mr Kat ran on to the stage. He beamed at Amelia as he snatched her microphone away. "Isn't she adorable! She's just like her puppy who stole my microphone when I was backstage. Full of mischief, the pair of them! But it's very naughty of you to tell fibs," Mr Kat continued. He gave Amelia a stern look. Then he reminded everyone of all the free things they could have if he became mayor.

Everyone clapped and cheered again.

Amelia's shoulders slumped. No matter how brave she'd been, Mr Kat had won.

The Paw Pad would close. Mr Kat would open a cat hotel. Then Mrs Springer, Alfie and her puppies would become homeless.

The crowd clapped for ages, but when they fell silent a voice called out.

"My name is Mrs Springer and I'm the owner of the Paw Pad. Mr Kat has been trying to make me sell it to him for ages. I've got emails that prove it. Everything Amelia told you is true. Mr Kat hates dogs. He is planning to ban dogs from Barkington. He wants everyone to get a cat and make him rich when he turns the Paw Pad into a cat hotel."

Mr Kat turned an angry shade of purple. Through gritted teeth, he said, "So what if I hate dogs? Cats are much nicer. They don't whine, dribble or steal your socks. People will thank me when they've swapped their dog for a cat. I'll give a handsome discount to any Barkington cat owner who wants to use my luxury cat hotel." Raising his voice, he faced the crowd. "Free parking, free popcorn and ice cream! No more smelly, dirty dogs! You'll still vote for me, won't you?"

Everyone stared silently back. An official came on to the stage.

"Ladies, gentlemen, children and dogs, Mr Kat has just been disqualified from running for mayor for being dishonest. But for now, the dog show must continue – and I know who my vote would go to." He smiled at Amelia, Alfie and the judge before he left the stage.

The judge took back the microphone. "We have a clear winner. I first noticed them backstage. The owner and dog who are most like each other, who work together and who have both shown huge amounts of courage today are Amelia and Alfie. Congratulations."

Before Amelia collected her trophy, she bent to give Alfie another big hug. They'd done it! Together they'd saved the Paw Pad.

"Thank you," she whispered in his ear. "I'd never have had the courage to speak out today without you. And I'm sorry for getting cross with you. You don't mean to be a mischievous nuisance. You just need someone to show you how to behave. That's my job and I've let you down."

Alfie snuggled against Amelia's leg, as if to say he forgave her.

When Amelia and Alfie left the stage, they were surrounded by Kelly, Anushka and Jack. Everyone wanted to congratulate them.

"Please say you'll hang out with us at school," said Kelly. "We've been trying to make friends with you and Alfie, but you keep running off."

Amelia couldn't stop grinning. "I'd love to hang out with you," she said, smiling.

"Cool – see you tomorrow!" said Kelly.

Amelia skipped back to her parents with Alfie. Mum and Dad were beaming too.

"Well done, Amelia!" said Dad. "We are so proud of you for overcoming your shyness to speak up for what you know was right."

"Mrs Springer asked us to thank you too," said Mum. "When I saw you talking to your new school friends, I took the opportunity to ask her if she would take Alfie back. She agreed that she would tomorrow. She's not open today."

"Oh!" said Amelia. Her heart flopped. She hadn't given Alfie a fair chance and now she was having second thoughts about her decision to return him.

A cold, wet nose nudged her. Blinking to stop the tears, Amelia put her hand down. Alfie licked it.

Amelia was very quiet on the way home. She spent the rest of the afternoon playing with Alfie in the garden and teaching him some simple commands. Alfie was a fast learner and he soon knew how to sit and stay. Best of all, though, was teaching him to raise his paw. Amelia loved how cute he looked when he high-fived her.

When Amelia went to bed, Alfie followed her upstairs, jumped on the bed and curled up next to her.

Alfie fell asleep quickly, but Amelia lay

awake, her arm round his plump velvety body, listening to his soft snores.

"Best day ever," she said softly. She'd saved the Paw Pad and made three new friends. She couldn't have done it without Alfie. But Alfie was going back to the Paw Pad tomorrow.

Unable to sleep, Amelia stared at the ceiling and thought about Alfie.

★★★

Someone was licking her ear! Amelia was jolted awake by a rough tongue. Sleepily, she rolled over. "Alfie!"

Alfie licked her nose, as if to say hello.

"Amelia, it's time to get up." Mum came into her room. "Wake up, sleepyhead. If you don't hurry, you'll be late for school and I will be late too. I'm taking Alfie back to the Paw Pad today."

Amelia pulled Alfie closer. "Does he have to go?"

Mum looked bewildered. "You said you didn't want to keep him."

"That was before," said Amelia, her heart thudding. "It's not Alfie's fault that he's naughty. He's just a baby. Alfie's much braver than me. He's not shy and he forced me to join in with things when I didn't want to. Mrs Springer was right. He really is my perfect puppy."

Alfie grunted, as if to say he agreed. He lifted his paw up and Amelia high-fived him. Mum laughed.

"I'm sure Mrs Springer will be delighted to hear that you've changed your mind. I'll ring her now," she said as she hurried away.

At breakfast, Amelia shared her toast crusts with Alfie. Then, as they walked to school with Mum, Amelia taught him to sit at the kerb and wait for the cars to pass before crossing. When the school came into view, Amelia's tummy wibbled like frogspawn. What if Kelly, Anushka and Jack had changed their minds and didn't want her to hang out with them after all?

"Hey, Amelia!"

"Amelia, wait up!"

"Alfie, wait for us!"

Amelia turned round to see Kelly, Anushka and Jack running to catch up with her. They were grinning from ear to ear as they bent to stroke Alfie.

"Alfie! Don't eat that!" Kelly burst out laughing as he swiped her homework from out of her bag.

Amelia dug into her pocket.

"Alfie, leave," she said, exchanging the treat for the homework and giving it back to Kelly. Luckily, the homework was only a little bit chewed.

"Bye, Mum. Bye, Alfie," Amelia said as she hugged them both goodbye.

Alfie licked her hand. Then Amelia, linking arms with her new friends, went into school.

Look out for more

Perfect Puppies

adventures

Six fun facts about puppies!

🐾 All puppies are born with blue eyes.

🐾 Puppies are born with a single layer of fur which they keep until they are 4–6 months old. Then they shed it to make way for their adult coats which are thicker.

🐾 Puppies can spend up to *twenty* hours a day sleeping!

🐾 Puppies don't open their eyes until they are around 13 days old.

🐾 Puppies are born with nails but no teeth.

🐾 Puppies sweat through their paws.

Can you find the hidden words within this word search?

A	T	S	A	P	I	D	W	L	O
C	F	R	B	L	Q	A	P	K	Z
O	A	C	E	K	J	L	Y	H	V
L	W	B	M	A	H	F	A	P	L
L	D	K	N	Y	T	I	J	W	E
A	P	Q	H	G	F	E	K	Q	A
R	L	Z	T	D	S	O	M	S	D
B	I	V	L	P	A	W	P	A	D
G	Y	N	S	B	X	L	N	C	J
X	D	P	U	P	P	Y	R	B	G

- Puppy
- Lead
- Treat
- Alfie
- Collar
- Paw Pad

Can you find Alfie by following the right lead?

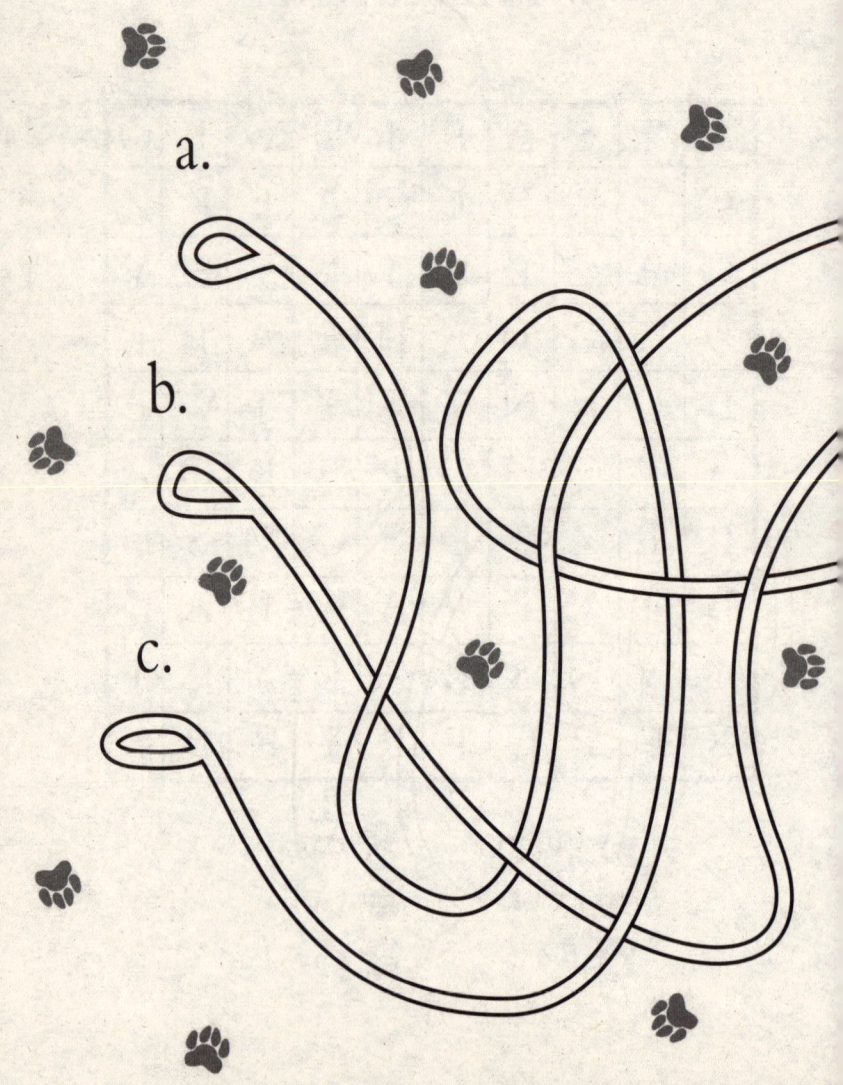

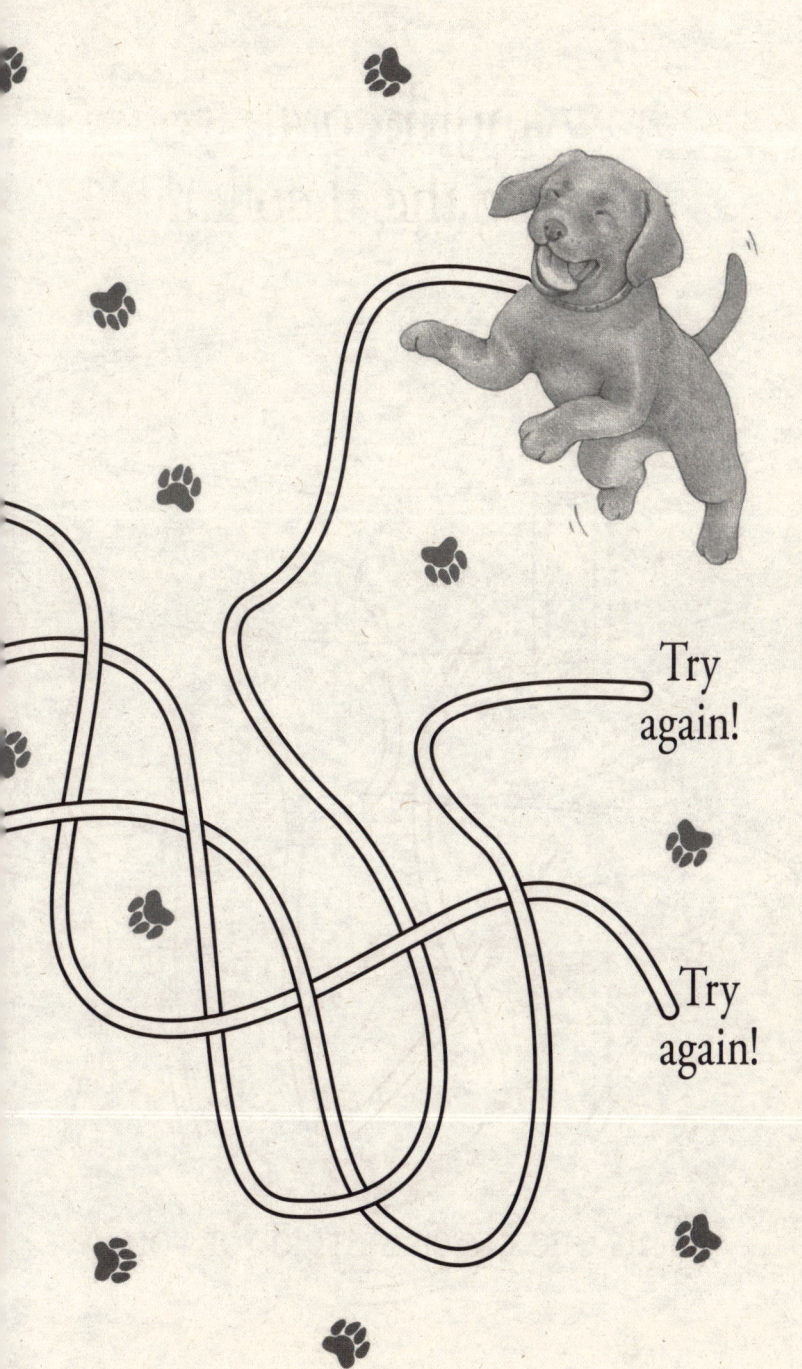

Draw and decorate your own magical collar!

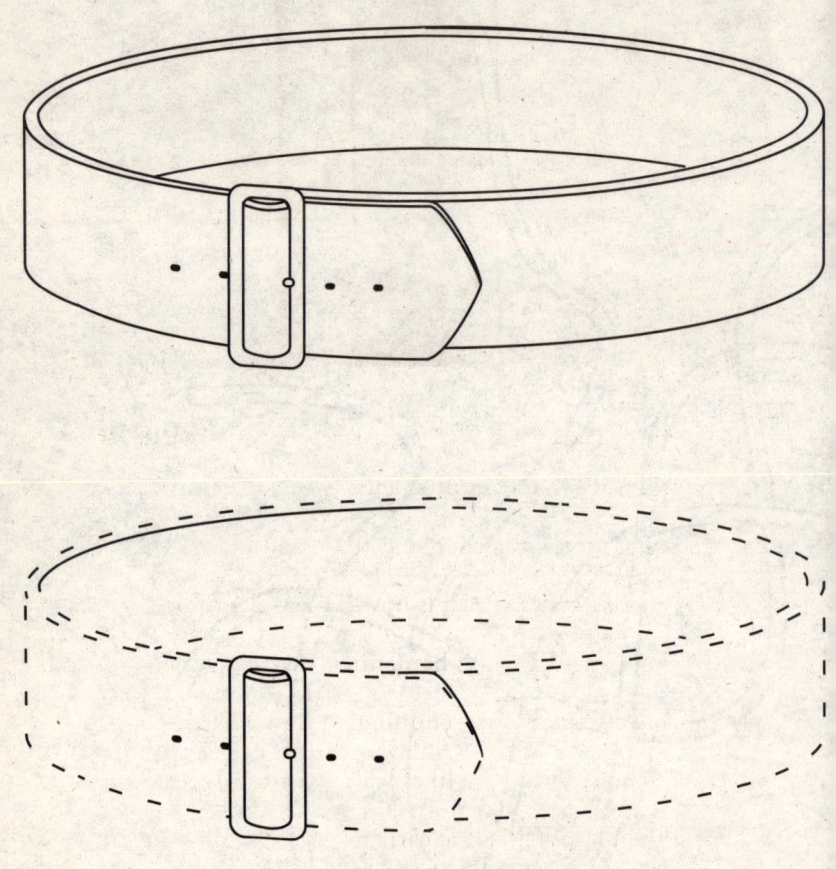

This one's been started for you.

About the Author

Julie Sykes is an award-winning author of over one hundred books for children. She is the co-author of the *Unicorn Academy* series which is now a Netflix animation. Julie lives in Cornwall with her family, two energetic sprollies and a white wolf – cunningly disguised as a dog. When she's not writing she likes walking, reading, eating cake and flying on her magic carpet. You can find out more about her at www.juliesykes.co.uk